THE KENNEDYS

END OF A DYNASTY

THE
KENNEDYS

END OF A DYNASTY

E Books

OR Robert Sullivan
CTOR OF PHOTOGRAPHY Barbara Baker Burrows
JTY PICTURE EDITOR Christina Lieberman
TIVE DIRECTOR Mimi Park
GNER Michael Roseman
OR WRITER Danny Freedman
ER-REPORTERS Marilyn Fu, Carol Vinzant
 EDITORS Danielle Dowling, Barbara Gogan, Parlan McGaw
SULTING PICTURE EDITORS Arnold Horton, Mimi Murphy (Rome),
Skari (Paris)
IAL THANKS Crary Pullen

SIDENT Andrew Blau
NESS MANAGER Roger Adler
NESS DEVELOPMENT MANAGER Jeff Burak

 INC. HOME ENTERTAINMENT
ISHER Richard Fraiman
RAL MANAGER Steven Sandonato
UTIVE DIRECTOR, MARKETING SERVICES Carol Pittard
CTOR, RETAIL & SPECIAL SALES Tom Mifsud
CTOR, NEW PRODUCT DEVELOPMENT Peter Harper
STANT DIRECTOR, BOOKAZINE MARKETING Laura Adam
STANT PUBLISHING DIRECTOR, BRAND MARKETING Joy Butts
CIATE COUNSEL Helen Wan
 PRODUCTION MANAGER Susan Janso
GN & PREPRESS MANAGER Anne-Michelle Gallero
D MANAGER Roshni Patel

RIAL OPERATIONS Richard K. Prue (Director), Brian Fellows (Manager),
 Aurelio, Charlotte Coco, John Goodman, Kevin Hart, Norma Jones,
Kerimoglu, Rosalie Khan, Patricia Koh, Marco Lau, Brian Mai,
ng Ng, Lorenzo Pace, Rudi Papiri, Robert Pizaro, Barry Pribula,
Renauro, Donald Schaedtler, Hia Tan, Vaune Trachtman, David Weiner

IAL THANKS Christine Austin, Glenn Buonocore, Jim Childs,
n Chodakiewicz, Rose Cirrincione, Jacqueline Fitzgerald, Lauren Hall,
fer Jacobs, Brynn Joyce, Mona Li, Robert Marasco, Amy Migliaccio,
ke Reger, Dave Rozzelle, Ilene Schreider, Adriana Tierno,
Voznesenskiy, Sydney Webber, Jonathan White

shed by LIFE Books

Inc.
Avenue of the Americas
York, NY 10020

13: 978-1-60320-132-2
10: 1-60320-132-7
y of Congress Control Number: 2009935972

elcome your comments and suggestions about LIFE Books.
e write to us at:
Books
ion: Book Editors
x 11016
loines, IA 50336-1016

 would like to order any of our hardcover
tor's Edition books, please call us at 1-800-327-6388
lay through Friday, 7:00 a.m.–8:00 p.m.,
urday, 7:00 a.m.–6:00 p.m., Central Time).

Us at **LIFE.com**

 put, this site has the most amazing collection of professional
graphy on the Web, with millions of iconic images
IFE magazine's archives, never-before-seen LIFE pictures and
-the-minute news photos. Come see for yourself!

PERS: Delegates listen as an ailing Senator Ted Kennedy provides
ing start to the 2008 Democratic National Convention in Denver.
raph by Max Whittaker/Getty

: Jack supports brother Teddy, while Bobby kneels, circa 1935.
raph courtesy of John F. Kennedy Library/Polaris

2–3: Ted Kennedy in a portrait made for LIFE in 1969.
raph by John Loengard

GE: Joseph P. Kennedy is surrounded by grandchildren
home in Hyannis Port, Massachusetts, in 1965.
raph courtesy of Kennedy Family Album

CONTENTS

A Family Like No Other

American dynasties are rare in the extreme, and among them no family name stirs emotion in our time as does that of Kennedy. We were reminded of this anew with the death, on August 25, 2009, at 77 years old, of Edward Moore Kennedy, the last surviving brother of the clan's storied generation—a generation that included, among nine siblings, Joe Jr. and Jack and Bobby and Eunice, the latter of whom predeceased Ted by precisely two weeks. A chapter

THEIR GREATEST GENERATION
When Joseph P. Kennedy Sr. was the U.S. ambassador to Great Britain from 1938 to 1940, his nine children bore the sunniest visages in London. From left: Eunice, Jack, Rosemary, Jean Ann, the patriarch Joe, Ted, the matriarch Rose, Joe Jr., Pat, Bobby and Kick. With Ted's death, only Jean Ann survives.

EVERETT COLLECTION/REX USA

in a thunderous saga neared its end with the passing of these two celebrated Americans, a chapter that featured the very greatest triumphs and the darkest tragedies, the most magnificent contributions and most egregious missteps.

In pondering the Kennedys once again, we found ourselves freshly amazed by the scope of their story. To say you couldn't have made it up is to say the very least; it's a narrative in every sense as mythic and dramatic as the American dream itself. They rose from the nation's great immigrant stock to grasp opportunity after opportunity, and when one generation conquered its own poverty and pulled the family up into the stratosphere of class, the next turned to

the suffering, the poor, the less fortunate they had left behind and used their newfound advantages as a fulcrum to turn the wheels of social justice. In the meantime: foibles and failures aplenty. The Kennedys' story is one that is as messy as it is glamorous, as strained and scarred by immorality, excess and fault as it is elevated by valor, righteousness and selflessness.

If Eunice was an exemplary Kennedy—giving, engaged, bright, energetic—then Ted was a Kennedy through and through, which is to say he was all of the above and also flawed. He stumbled personally and this affected him professionally, which was a shame because, as a U.S. senator, he was enormously successful and effective—and who knows how he might have performed in an even higher office? None of the biographies of the most famous Kennedys is either linear or clean. Joseph Kennedy Sr., patriarch of those who ascended politically, was notoriously amoral in his quest for power. Jack, the gleaming King Arthur of America's Camelot, has been revealed posthumously as a vain and selfish man, an unfaithful husband to the woman his countrymen came to idolize, Jackie. Bobby could be ruthless and calculating, and Ted—as said, and as we will see—had his own demons.

But they all cared so much, worked so hard and achieved such things for their country that we don't quite know how to parse this story. Imagine: a single family rising from the very most humble of American origins, the immigrant slum class, and making its way through grinding poverty to ascend, in barely a century, to a position where it would impact, and perhaps better, the day-to-day living of all its fellow Americans. This the Kennedys—and no other clan in the history of our country—did. This they achieved. And it is a remarkable achievement.

Ted's death asked us to look at the Kennedys again, and that's a good thing. With his exit, there are no Kennedys in the Senate for the first time since 1962; if you figure that Jack was in the White House that year and extend his own Senate service backward from 1960 when he was elected President, then it's more than half a century that the Kennedys have been holding high office in this country. They were, as we will see, influencing Boston and Massachusetts even longer ago. To total their contributions would be impossible; to attempt to do so would prove as fruitless as would any effort to catalog their sins.

The Kennedys are not done, not by any means. On the following pages is a family tree; it extends to the children of Ted and Jack and Bobby's generation, but no further. There are scores more young Kennedys out there today, all of them tracing their roots to the four famine refugees: Patrick and Bridget Kennedy, and Thomas and Rose Anna Fitzgerald. The newest Kennedys each know that they have a torch to carry and a responsibility. How they might rise is anyone's guess.

But today, Ted Kennedy is gone—and thus ends an era. Thus ends a dynasty.

Perhaps it was the *first* Kennedy dynasty. Only tomorrow knows.

■ **Patrick Kennedy**
b. 1823   *d.* 1858

m. 1849
■ **Bridget Murphy**
b. 1821(?)   *d.* 1888

■ **Patrick Joseph Kennedy**
(and four siblings)
b. 1858   *d.* 1929

m. 1887
■ **Mary Augusta Hickey**
b. 1857   *d.* 1923

■ **Joseph Patrick Kennedy**
(and three siblings)
b. 1888   *d.* 1969

CORBIS

■ **Joseph Patrick Kennedy Jr.**
b. 1915   *d.* 1944

GETTY

■ **John Fitzgerald Kennedy**
b. 1917   *d.* 1963

m. 1953
■ **Jacqueline Lee Bouvier**
b. 1929   *d.* 1994

CORBIS

■ **Rose Marie ("Rosemary") Kennedy**
b. 1918   *d.* 2005

CORBIS

■ **Kathleen Agnes Kennedy**
b. 1920   *d.* 1948

m. 1944
■ **William John Robert Cavendish, Marquess of Hartington**
b. 1917   *d.* 1944

■ **Arabella Kennedy**
b. 1956   *d.* 1956
■ **Caroline Bouvier Kennedy**
b. 1957
■ **John Fitzgerald Kennedy Jr.**
b. 1960   *d.* 1999
■ **Patrick Bouvier Kennedy**
b. 1963   *d.* 1963

■ First Generation
■ Second Generation
■ Third Generation
■ Fourth Generation
■ Fifth Generation
■ Spouses

THE FAMILY TREE

HAL PHYFE

■ **Thomas Fitzgerald**
b. 1823   *d.* 1885
m. 1857
■ **Rose Anna Cox**
b. 1835   *d.* 1879

■ **John Francis Fitzgerald**
(and 11 siblings)
b. 1863   *d.* 1950

m. 1884
■ **Mary Josephine Hannon**
b. 1865   *d.* 1964

m. 1914

■ **Rose Elizabeth Fitzgerald**
(and five siblings)
b. 1890   *d.* 1995

■ **Eunice Mary Kennedy**
b. 1921   *d.* 2009
m. 1953
■ **Robert Sargent Shriver Jr.**
b. 1915

■ **Patricia Kennedy**
b. 1924   *d.* 2006
m. 1954   *div.* 1966
■ **Peter Lawford**
b. 1923   *d.* 1984

■ **Robert Francis Kennedy**
b. 1925   *d.* 1968
m. 1950
■ **Ethel Skakel**
b. 1928

■ **Jean Ann Kennedy**
b. 1928
m. 1956
■ **Stephen Edward Smith**
b. 1927   *d.* 1990

■ **Edward Moore Kennedy**
b. 1932   *d.* 2009
m. 1958   *div.* 1982
■ **Virginia Joan Bennett**
b. 1936

m. 1992
■ **Victoria Anne Reggie**
b. 1954

■ **Robert Sargent Shriver III**
b. 1954
■ **Maria Owings Shriver**
b. 1955
■ **Timothy Perry Shriver**
b. 1959
■ **Mark Kennedy Shriver**
b. 1964
■ **Anthony Paul Kennedy Shriver**
b. 1965

■ **Christopher Kennedy Lawford**
b. 1955
■ **Sydney Maleia Kennedy Lawford**
b. 1956
■ **Victoria Francis Lawford**
b. 1958
■ **Robin Elizabeth Lawford**
b. 1961

■ **Kathleen Hartington Kennedy**
b. 1951
■ **Joseph Patrick Kennedy II**
b. 1952
■ **Robert Francis Kennedy Jr.**
b. 1954
■ **David Anthony Kennedy**
b. 1955   *d.* 1984
■ **Mary Courtney Kennedy**
b. 1956
■ **Michael LeMoyne Kennedy**
b. 1958   *d.* 1997
■ **Mary Kerry Kennedy**
b. 1959
■ **Christopher George Kennedy**
b. 1963
■ **Matthew Maxwell Taylor Kennedy**
b. 1965
■ **Douglas Harriman Kennedy**
b. 1967
■ **Rory Elizabeth Katherine Kennedy**
b. 1968

■ **Stephen Edward Smith Jr.**
b. 1957
■ **William Kennedy Smith**
b. 1960
■ **Amanda Mary Smith**
b. 1967
■ **Kym Maria Smith**
b. 1972

■ **Kara Anne Kennedy**
b. 1960
■ **Edward Moore Kennedy Jr.**
b. 1961
■ **Patrick Joseph Kennedy**
b. 1967

Dynasty
THE KENNEDYS IN AMERICA

P ATRICK KENNEDY, AN IMMIGRANT TO the United States who fled Ireland during the Great Famine of the mid-19th century, was the patriarch of what grew to be certainly the most remarkable (adherents would argue, greatest) of all Irish American families. Bridget Murphy, too, was a famine refugee—from the same county, Wexford, as Kennedy. She traveled to America aboard the same ship in 1849. She would become his wife and thus the matriarch of that family.

Eighteen forty-nine, not the legendary Black '47, was in fact the worst year of the famine. As Terry Golway tells us in his book *The Irish in America*, Patrick, 26, was part of a family that farmed 25 acres in Dunganstown. His elder brother, John, had died years earlier, and Patrick left behind his parents, one brother and a sister, making his way to Liverpool, where he boarded the *Washington Irving*, a vessel named for the first American writer of international reputation. Family legend held that aboard ship, Patrick met Bridget, and they found they had a month to kill and much in common to discuss. By the time the boat reached Boston, they were in love.

Patrick and Bridget married. The newlywed Kennedys had not arrived in any way rich and took up residence in the slum of East Boston—they probably couldn't afford the two-penny ferry to cross the harbor into downtown. Their quarters were in a precinct where, as Golway put it, "children were born to die." The conditions in the "Paddyvilles" were beyond deplorable; Golway pointed out that 60 percent of those born in Boston at that time didn't live to see their sixth birthday, and "adults fared little better, for the average Famine immigrant lived no longer than five or six years after stepping foot on American soil. The Irish lived in shanties and basements, breeding grounds of disease and despair. A Boston doctor was visiting a patient lying ill in a bedroom filled with water when a tiny coffin floated by. It contained the body of the patient's child."

Patrick became a cooper. Bridget bore three daughters and two sons, one of whom would not survive, in eight years (a pace that would seem plodding to the family of Robert and Ethel Kennedy a century later). In doing his research, Golway found a public health

IN P.J.'S FOOTSTEPS
Above: Patrick Joseph Kennedy, son of Patrick and Bridget, in a photograph taken circa 1880, a few years before he married Mary Augusta Hickey in 1887. In 1888, their son Joseph, pictured here at age two (right), was born. Something that P.J. could never have dreamed of but that Joe strove for vigorously throughout his entire adult life came to pass on November 8, 1960: A member of their clan was elected President of the United States of America. The group photo at left was taken on the evening after that great triumph at the home of the victor, John F. Kennedy. Seated in the front row are Eunice Kennedy Shriver; Rose, the matriarch of this generation of Kennedys, whose maiden name was Fitzgerald; Rose's husband, Joe, who is dressed in a far more

conventional manner than he was at two years old; Jackie, the President-elect's wife; and Ted. Back row: Ethel, Bobby's wife; Stephen Smith and his wife, Jean Kennedy Smith; JFK himself; Bobby; Pat Kennedy Lawford; Sargent Shriver, husband of Eunice; Joan, wife of Ted; and Peter Lawford, Pat's husband. This is the extended version of America's new First Family.

THE FLAMBOYANT FITZGERALDS

In the photograph from a family locket at top are John F. "Honey Fitz" and Mary Josephine Fitzgerald. Among their children were (above, from left) Agnes, Tom and Rose. We say "the flamboyant Fitzgeralds," but we speak primarily of Honey Fitz. He was a backslapping Irish pol of phenomenal reputation; his gift of the gab gave rise to the term "Fitzblarney" locally and inspired a contemporaneous bit of doggerel that ran "Honey Fitz can talk you blind / On any subject you can find / Fish and fishing, motor boats / Railroads, streetcars, getting votes."

commission report from approximately the time when Patrick and Bridget were raising their children: "Huddled together like brutes, without regard to sex or age, or sense of decency; grown men and women sleeping together in the same apartment, and sometimes wife and husband, brothers and sisters in the same bed . . . self-respect, forethought, all high and noble virtues soon die out [replaced by] sullen indifference and despair, or disorder, intemperance and utter degradation."

Cholera hit these Irish slums hard, killing hundreds, including Patrick. He left behind one son to carry his name, his last-born child, Patrick Joseph Kennedy.

The boy, "P.J.," went to school under the Sisters of Notre Dame, worked in Boston Harbor as a stevedore, saved some money, borrowed some from his mother and took possession of a saloon in a dilapidated part of town. He worked hard, his bar prospered and, still in his twenties, he was able to buy into two more establishments. By the age of 30, he had formed his own liquor-importing business, P.J. Kennedy and Company. He married up in class, catching, in 1887, Mary Augusta Hickey—daughter of a businessman and sister of a police lieutenant, a physician who had graduated from Harvard, and a funeral director.

P.J. and Mary would have two sons (the second would die in infancy) and two daughters. Their first-born, in 1888, was given an inversion of the family name: Joseph Patrick Kennedy. Bridget Kennedy lived to see her grandchild Joe born on September 6 but died before the year was out at age 67.

Little Joe would grow to be quite a piece of work.

I N THE MEANTIME, JAMES FITZGERALD, when only 10 or 11 years old, also fled the famine, leaving Limerick, in the west of Ireland, and arriving in America in (or just after) 1848, accompanied by an uncle and a cousin. He got terribly sick during the crossing and was sheltered by his kin under a blanket lest the captain think he had typhus and throw him overboard. A ferocious storm battered the ship as it neared the U.S. coast. It is not known for certain but could be true: The ship may have been heading for New York City and was blown off course to Boston; fate may have played a larger role than is evident in the powerful coming together of the Fitzgeralds and the Kennedys.

According to Doris Kearns Goodwin in her biographical history of these two seminal Irish families, James, of all the Fitzgerald children who eventually immigrated, "adapted the most readily to the challenge of life in the New World. Whereas his sisters and brothers retained all their lives many characteristics of western Ireland, James, with his ready will and raw intelligence, made himself thoroughly comfortable in the city." James clerked in a store that he eventually bought and turned, during a half-century's proprietorship, into a great success. At 20, he, too, married up, to Julia Adeline Brophy. Once he brought his brother Thomas into the business, he was able to expand his store to stock liquor and open an adjunct saloon. The Fitzgerald place at 310 North Street became the neighborhood local as well as the country store. Thomas's wife, Rose Anna, also came to work in the store.

Thomas and Rose Anna had 12 children in all; John Francis Fitzgerald, born in 1863, was the fourth boy among them. (While James's family slowly became one of the very wealthiest in Boston's North End, Thomas's grew to be stable and safe—no small victory.) "John Fitzgerald long relished the memory of good food . . . he spoke of eating fish as well as meat and of having fresh vegetables every day," wrote Goodwin, "and he particularly remembered Sunday nights when his mother made flapjacks which he loved to drown in butter and syrup or molasses.

"If the store did well by day, it thrived by night as the neighborhood men, home from a long day of hard work, began to drop in for drinks."

Thomas was able, by 1866, to buy a three-story tenement for his burgeoning family on Hanover

Street (cost: $6,550). He opened his own grocery on the ground floor and became a landlord, buying two more tenements to rent out. And the family grew and grew—nine boys in all, three of whom would prosper as their father had in the liquor business, three of whom were heavy drinkers and died young. "The curse of the liquor money," one relative mourned.

Johnny, the most diminutive, was perhaps the most determined of the bunch; he would remember much later, "We used to run on the sidewalks and cobblestones of Hanover Street, and I could always beat any of the boys. I could also sprint around the loop of old Fort Hill in a shorter time than any competitors. As a sprinter my distance was from 120 to 150 yards. I won the half mile distance cup in Boston in one year. I was a champ." We cite this with emphasis: Between his uncle James's charm and Johnny's own vibrancy, it becomes clear that many of the instinctual traits that the family would become famous for were forming, very early on, in the side of the clan named not Kennedy but Fitzgerald.

It was Johnny, as opposed to his two surviving older brothers, who emerged as a leader: "For some reason, it was my trust to boss the family." He was remembered by his kin as "the one who taught the others how to swim, how to play ball and how to whistle through their fingers." He was the one "who kept the whole family together."

In 1877, 14-year-old Johnny was selling newspapers on Boston's streets. It wasn't a bad gig at all: He could make $2.50 a week. Arriving in the predawn to pick up his papers, he fell in love with the business and the bustle of the newsroom. He made friends there and throughout the city. Everyone loved seeing Johnny Fitzgerald. Everything was grand.

In 1879, his mother, Rose Anna, died of a stroke. Thomas Fitzgerald, having lost a young daughter to cholera, two other children in infancy and now his wife—who was pregnant when she died—to a brain malady, determined that one of his nine sons should become a doctor. And so it was that John, the leader, was sent to Boston Latin School and then to Harvard Medical School. In 1885, Thomas Fitzgerald died of pneumonia at 62. John, parentless in his early twenties, was thoroughly a man—married to the former Mary Josephine "Josie" Hannon, respected by all, a promising newcomer in ward politics. John and Josie named their

BETTMANN/CORBIS

first daughter, born on a hot and steamy July 22, 1890, Rose Elizabeth. LIFE's Brad Darrach, upon Rose Kennedy's death more than a century later, would be able to look back and write without undue hyperbole, "She was the Queen Mother of Camelot. A tribal matriarch as formidable as the iron-willed dam of the Bonapartes, she bore and nurtured America's most dazzling political dynasty. Yet she saw, one after another, five of her nine children—three of her four sons—struck down in a family tragedy as grim as any Shakespeare contrived."

JOE ON THE RISE

P.J. Kennedy had succeeded to the point that his offspring would be given advantages. Here we see his son Joe circa 1907 as captain of Company B, the military drill team at the esteemed Boston Latin School. Joe was president of his class, too, and would soon be Harvard bound.

JOHN FITZGERALD CONTINUED TO DO exceedingly well. He had an innate talent for politics, and soon the press was calling him "the Little Napoleon of Ward 6," as he consolidated support among the Irish as well as the newer Italian and Russian immigrants who had followed into Boston. His personal machine was called the Jefferson Club, and it helped him get elected, first to the city's Common Council, then to the state senate. The *Boston Daily Advertiser* cited him as "the most called for man at the state-house." In 1894, Fitzgerald set his sights on the U.S. congressional seat that would become the dominion in the second half of the 20th century of John F. Kennedy, House Speaker Tip O'Neill and Joseph P. Kennedy II. It was, in Fitzgerald's day, the only Democratic district in

IRISH ROSE
Rose is in the foreground at left, her father is aft. Above: She and the waggish mayor of Boston are about to embark on a tour of South America. Rose led a youthful life on the go as her father's political dance partner, being whisked off to meetings with the President in Washington, D.C., then to great cities an ocean away. As for Honey Fitz's demure wife, Josie, she was the family's rock. "I am a home woman in every way," she once said. "And my one ambition is to make the home a most happy and attractive place for my husband and children."

Massachusetts, and he would have to upset a fellow Irish American, Joseph O'Neil, who was a favorite of several city bosses, including P.J. Kennedy. The Wall Street panic of 1893, however, had created unrest, and all incumbents were suddenly vulnerable. Fitzgerald appealed to the poor and unemployed, and the economic depression carried him to victory. "Now that the fight is over, P.J., let's shake hands," a tired Fitzgerald offered on the morning after his primary election win to the ward boss Kennedy. They did, and Fitzgerald got the Boston machine behind him.

Fitzgerald's family stayed in Massachusetts while he went to Washington. The brood had grown—Rose had a sister, Agnes, and a brother, Thomas, by now—and Josie coped by moving them all to West Concord. "These were wonderful years," Rose would recall, "full of the traditional pleasures and satisfactions of life in a small New England town: trips with horse and buggy to my grandparents' house, climbing apple trees, gathering wildflowers in the woods behind the house."

There were vacations north of Concord. The Fitzgeralds encamped each summer in a cottage in Old Orchard Beach, Maine, one of the several "Irish Rivieras"—like Spring Lake, New Jersey, or Hampton Beach, New Hampshire—that were being established on the Atlantic seaboard by families on the rise. There, in 1895, Rose met a seven-year-old named Joseph Patrick Kennedy, who was also vacationing with his parents.

John Fitzgerald came home for good in 1900, saying he didn't want to run for Congress again. He had bought a Catholic weekly newspaper earlier, and it had done well, so now he had the money for a mansion in Dorchester. The family moved back in toward the Hub and, in 1905, after the incumbent mayor of Boston had died on vacation, Fitzgerald entered a three-way horse race and won.

Rose would turn 16 in the summer of '06, and she again met Joe Kennedy at Old Orchard Beach. Joe and Rose were their fathers' children, as smart, confident, energetic and optimistic as either P.J. Kennedy or John Fitzgerald, and that's saying something. Rose remembered later that young Joe—class president and captain of the baseball team at Boston Latin—had "the most wonderful smile that seemed to light up his entire face from within and made an instant impression on everyone he met." Hers wasn't bad either. As

SUMMER LOVE
On the sands of Old Orchard Beach in Maine, Rose and Joe met as kids and fell for each other as teenagers—to the consternation of Rose's father. The photograph at left couldn't have been staged better: In 1907, Rose is third from left, Joe is second from right and Rose's dad is right in the center (fourth from left)—almost literally trying to come between them. But to no avail, and on October 7, 1914, after a courtship of seven years, Rose made a lovely bride (above). A final identification: P.J. Kennedy, Joe's father, is second from left at Old Orchard.

DEAR HYANNIS PORT
Joe and Rose's brood now numbers eight, and Teddy is on the way; he would be born in 1932. Upon graduating from Harvard in 1912, Joe had decided to eschew the family trade—politics—and go into finance. He already had some experience with successful enterprises: He had hawked candy as a kid, and in college he was an operator and part owner of a sightseeing tour bus. He continued to be a precocious titan of business and was a bank president by age 25. With their burgeoning wealth, the Kennedys were able to buy property in what would become their clan's spiritual home, Hyannis Port on Cape Cod in Massachusetts.

Darrach wrote in LIFE: "At 16 she was a magical creature—elegant, spirited, well read." But summers never last forever. Joe went on to Harvard, and Rose to a convent school in the Netherlands.

Rose had been nicknamed "Father Says" for her often-repeated phrase, but she disobeyed the elder Fitzgerald, now known to all as "Honey Fitz," by secretly dating Joseph Kennedy when she was home (the Kennedys weren't high society enough, Honey Fitz insisted). Rose eventually profited from her father's errant ways. After rumors leaked out about Dad's dalliance with a Boston cigarette girl named Toodles, Rose wed Joe in 1914—and who would dare say anything about it? Rose's life was being formed in both her parents' images. From the Boston pol she got brains and charm, from the matriarch she got her black-Irish loveliness, her genes for longevity (Josie would live to be 98; Rose, 104) and her avid Catholicism, reinforced by her convent training. "Freed from all distractions and from all worldly

thoughts," she once said, "I was able to find in myself the place that was meant for God." This stoic faith would see her through when husband Joe, too, took up with his various Toodleses down the years.

IF ROSE'S SPIRITUAL BELIEFS HELPED hold this troubled marriage together for so many years, another bond was her and Joe's shared ambitions. They imagined, and wanted, the world for their young Kennedys.

The firstborn, Joe Jr., was to be President. He was raised that way at home by Rose and from afar by Joe Sr., who was often away earning millions for the family in the stock market, in Hollywood (where the famous affairs come in—including the one with Gloria Swanson) and in the age-old Kennedy-Fitzgerald concern, liquor (even when it was outlawed during Prohibition). "The molding of the family was largely left to Rose," wrote Darrach in LIFE, "and she did an astonishing job. She organized the household like a small town and ran it like a mayor, supervising a staff of cooks, nannies, maids and secretaries. She was the health department: She made sure teeth were brushed after every meal, drove the gang to the dentist every few weeks and kept a medical history of each child on file cards. She was the police department: She regularly whacked backsides with a coat hanger, as well as with a ruler. She was the religion teacher: She tried to take at least some of the kids to church every day and, after Sunday service, quizzed them about the sermon. She was the school system: She hired tennis, golf, swimming, skiing and skating instructors and gave tests at mealtimes ('What does the word "Florida" mean? When is the longest day of the year?') Above all, she taught responsibility (quoting Saint Luke, 'To whom much has been given, much will be required') and the supreme importance of winning ('No matter what you do, you should try to be first')." Kennedy drill sessions, at or after dinner, would become traditions in the families of her children as well.

Meanwhile, for herself, Rose went to Mass every day (she would continue to do so until crippled by a stroke at 93). Doris Kearns Goodwin recounted a story suggesting that during the marriage to Joe, Rose

adhered to a strict interpretation of Church teaching that defines the principal purpose of sex as procreation. Per this doctrine, sex is forbidden during pregnancy—and for 17 years Rose was pregnant about half the time. She had her last child at 41, and at that point, according to Goodwin's telling, she told Joe, "No more sex." But long before then, according to Darrach, "the fire had surely gone out: Rose and Joe took separate vacations and stayed in different hotels

when they did travel together. Joe became a chaser— a fact he kept secret from no one, including his sons." We mention these things only by way of explaining the difficulties within this magical family, a family that kept its focus and its dignified front even as there were problems behind the walls. We mention them also to imply that what "Joe's boys" saw at home surely must have influenced their philosophies regarding the rules of life.

MERRIE OLDE ENGLAND
The elegant digs at 14 Prince's Gate in London were the official residence of the U.S. ambassador to Great Britain when Joe was appointed to that post in 1938 and when this photograph of his wife and four of their children (from left, Teddy, Bobby, Kathleen and Rosemary) was taken at teatime.

A S SAID, THE CHILDREN OF ROSE AND Joe—all but one, with Ted's passing, now dead—began to be born. They were, in chronological order of appearance:

JOSEPH P. KENNEDY JR., who was even more handsome than his father (and as dazzlingly so as the next oldest brother, John, would prove to be). Joe, born on July 25, 1915, was the chosen one. Joe Sr. may have had dreams of the White House for himself, but scandal and bad politics—he had a bootlegger's reputation; he was seen as soft on fascism in the '30s; he was thought by some to be anti-Semitic; he was terribly slow to come around regarding America's intervention in World War II—doomed him. So it would be Joe Jr., in every way raised to be a junior Joe, who would fulfill the dream. Within the family, he was the designated leader, and it's a role he wanted and protected. Jack would tease him, and there was a lot of tussling between the two older boys. Jack refused to obey Joe's commands; Bobby remembered later that the others would cower as the two brothers went at it. (The stronger of the two, Joe would win the battles, but Jack was undeterred.) Joe might well have made it to the White House, but the fighter pilot's plane exploded in flight on August 12, 1944, and he was dead at 29. Robert F. Kennedy Jr., Bobby's son and Joe's nephew, once told LIFE in an interview, "That was always portrayed, in our family, not as the ultimate sacrifice, but as the ultimate extension of a life—to give yourself for our country. We were taught in our family to envy Joe."

JOHN FITZGERALD KENNEDY, who grew up without the pressure. Born on May 29, 1917, he had to confront no greater expectations than happiness and well-being for 27 years, and so he was free to form himself as a fun guy, a fair scholar, a lover of books (he listed toward adventure stories) and a willing supplicant to the fates (the hand they would deal him!). Joe Jr.'s domination of Jack caused the second child to become something of an anti-Joe: sloppy in his bedroom where Joe was orderly, lazy at school where Joe was industrious, carefree where Joe was intense. JFK did all the right things, however—Harvard, the service. He, like Joe, turned out to be a World War II hero (his valor aboard PT-109 is unquestioned, no matter

how his father subsequently blared the news). Then he turned out to be an impossibly charismatic congressional candidate. Then he turned out to be an electrifying President. Then he turned out to be the greatest American martyr since Abraham Lincoln. More on him in a moment.

THE BIG BOYS
Joe and Jack (opposite, from left, in 1925) and Jack and Joe (above, in 1944) were the always devoted, always competing leaders of the Kennedy pack.

She was diagnosed as mentally handicapped for reasons beyond the medical grasp of the day (a diagnosis that has since been openly doubted by some biographers). At a time of little understanding or compassion for the mentally challenged, the Kennedys remained determined to keep Rosemary at home. (She is seen at right with her father at the London Children's Zoo on a day in 1938 when her younger brothers, Bobby and Teddy, cut the ribbon at the official opening.) Rose and Joe made it a priority for Rosemary's siblings to look after and include her, and they provided her with a battery of tutors and coaches, while keeping her condition an airtight family secret until the 1960s. It is interesting that both of Rosemary's siblings who passed away in August of 2009, Eunice and Ted, were deeply inspired by their older sister: Eunice to found the Special Olympics, Ted to work tirelessly for the legal rights of the disabled.

BETTMANN/CORBIS

ROSEMARY KENNEDY, born September 13, 1918, a happy girl with a story that now reads sad. She had followed her two brothers to the Edward Devotion School for kindergarten, but the teachers could not recommend her for first grade. She was a lovely and sweet youngster, and yet observers were quickly saying that she was mentally handicapped. Had she suffered from the flu epidemic of '18? Perhaps. But no matter. She was a Kennedy and would be given the best care money could buy. By her early twenties, she had received all of that and was perhaps the most beautiful of any Kennedy woman before or since. And so her parents were concerned for her, and about her increasingly violent moods. A large problem was that in the 1920s and '30s, the understanding and treatment of mental disabilities was woefully unsophisticated. Her parents despaired. They worried for Rosemary's choices and her safety. Joe took matters into his own hands and, without informing Rose or anyone else in the family, had Rosemary lobotomized—a then new treatment for mental illness. "He thought it would help her," Rose would say when she herself was 90, speaking with bitterness. "But it made her go all the way back. It erased all those years of effort I had put into her. All along I had continued to believe that she could have lived her life as a Kennedy girl, just a little slower." In 1949, Rosemary went to live in an institution in Wisconsin, where she would reside until her death in 2005.

KICK

Smart, outgoing, compassionate and at ease among all her brothers and sisters, Kathleen was a picture of vivacity. As she had with all the other Kennedy daughters, Rose enrolled Kathleen in convent schools (while the boys instead attended prep academies), so imagine Mom's chagrin—her horror— when Kick fell hard for an Anglican Brit and married outside the Church. Rose was indeed put off, and there was a chilliness from some of the other superdevout Kennedys as well, but not from Kick's soul mate Jack (seen with her here in Palm Beach, Florida, in the 1930s). He was, in many ways, the male version of Kick and was devastated when he learned of her death in a plane crash in 1948.

KATHLEEN KENNEDY—later Kathleen Kennedy Cavendish, Marchioness of Hartington—born on February 20, 1920, married at 24 and dead at 28. "Kick" will be remembered as forever young. She was the spark, she was the kick of the Kennedys. Wrote Goodwin: "What set Kathleen apart from her siblings was the fact that she more than they maintained a sense of wonder at how lucky she was to be born who she was in her family and in the world." Again according to Goodwin, Joe Jr., Jack and Kick were "a family within the family . . . the golden trio." Kick and JFK were especially close and grew more so after Joe Jr.'s death. Kick was a female amalgamation of Joe Sr., Joe Jr. and John Fitzgerald (either one, JFK or Honey Fitz). All the men loved her, and when Joe Sr. was posted as ambassador to England early in World War II, she was, perhaps, the most sought-after woman on the island. Kathleen, although of course of Irish heritage, dearly loved England, and whether that increased her affection for William John Robert "Billy" Cavendish, ninth Marquess of Hartington, cannot now be said but only speculated. Suffice it to say, she did love and marry him. Billy died during the war, and Kick perished not long after, with her new love, in a plane crash. It was 1948, and the word arrived first in the United States at the office of Congressman John F. Kennedy, his sister's favorite.

EUNICE, PAT AND JEAN

Above: In the summer of 1939 at the ambassador's residence in London, Jack sees a camera and grabs the spotlight (as is his wont) away from his sister Eunice, whose 18th birthday is being celebrated this night. Opposite, left to right: Patricia, Dad and Jean Ann in 1938. Eunice assumed a stewardship post for her four younger siblings—Pat, Bobby, Jean and Teddy—and, as said earlier, maintained a close relationship, probably the closest of all, with Rosemary. She was a quiet leader and in another era might have emerged as the star of the family. Her father once remarked admiringly that if she had been born male—Joe employed a ripe vulgarity that we will decorously avoid here—"she would have been a hell of a politician." As it was, she achieved plenty, much more than many a pol, and bettered the lives of millions.

EUNICE MARY KENNEDY, born on July 10, 1921, a smart and sensible Kennedy, but nonetheless strong and vibrant. Though Kick was her idol—everyone loved Kick—young Eunice was caught between older and younger siblings, and found herself more often aligned with Pat and Bobby and, later, Jean and Teddy. Her health, like her brother Jack's, wasn't the best; she was plagued by chronic stomach troubles. But she had, like him, a capacity to ignore pain, and she didn't think of herself. "Somehow," a family friend told Doris Kearns Goodwin, "Eunice seemed to develop very early on a sense of special responsibility for Rosemary as if Rosemary were her child instead of her sister. There was an odd maturity about Eunice which was sometimes forbidding but which clearly set her off from all the rest." This trait would underlie the great accomplishments of her life. At 26, she was working for the Juvenile Delinquency Committee of the Justice Department and saying things like "substantial efforts must be made to keep adolescents from quitting school at 14 or 15 and to give them a chance to learn a trade or develop special skills." She was the strongest-minded of her generation and an instinctive politician (she was a great aid in 1960 during her older brother's national campaign). In May of 1953, she married Robert Sargent Shriver after a seven-year courtship. Shriver, who ran Joe's Merchandise Mart in Chicago, was also instrumental in forming the Peace Corps. For her part, Eunice Shriver founded the Special Olympics, which grew out of a summer camp on the lawns of the Shrivers' greater Washington, D.C., estate, and saw the organization grow to mammoth size, helping mentally handicapped children around the world. Eunice died just before Ted in the summer of 2009, and perhaps a sign of how dire his prospects had become was the fact that he could not attend his dear sister's services.

PATRICIA KENNEDY, born on May 6, 1924, a Kennedy in all ways, but quieter. She was taller, more lovely and more athletic than her sisters, but as Rose once observed, she never seemed "particularly ambitious or enthusiastic or keen about anything . . . She would never make the effort to achieve distinction." Perhaps she was overwhelmed by all the achieving-of-distinction going on around her. She found her own friends outside the clan and enjoyed their company. In June 1954, Pat, age 30, married the English actor Peter Lawford, and the following year they had the first of four children. The Lawford link is an interesting one: He was about to become a core member, along with Dean Martin, Joey Bishop and Sammy Davis Jr., of Frank Sinatra's wild-and-woolly Las Vegas–based Rat Pack. John F. Kennedy, never one to pass up a good time, would become an orbital associate of the Pack—"Chickie Baby," Sinatra called him—and would meet women through his association. He would also, as we'll see, gain needed assistance from these show-business stars during his run for the White House, both onstage and behind the scenes. Ultimately, Bobby Kennedy would counsel his brother to cut ties with Sinatra and Co., as unsavory things concerning the Mob were being said about the group. JFK would heed his brother's advice, and that would be it for poor Peter Lawford: banished from the Pack forever. No one could hold a grudge like Sinatra. Years after the snub by the Kennedys, he refused to take the stage at the Sands Hotel one night because he spotted Lawford in the audience. Not until the actor was removed would Sinatra sing. As for Pat Kennedy, she divorced the actor in 1966 and raised the children through their teenage years herself. Peter Lawford died in 1984; Pat never remarried and died in 2006.

"Bobby is like me," Joe Sr. once boasted, "hard as nails." The father had come a long way to arrive at that estimation. Rose once recalled that she and Joe initially fretted that Bobby would turn out "puny and girlish." But he proved to have great grit, determination and a solid moral core. On this page we see Bobby (left) and a school chum, John Sheffield, enjoying a curious Anglo-American meeting of the minds during the Kennedys' posting in London: It's the Fourth of July, so they're celebrating at a party at the American embassy, but doing so with the veddy British treat of strawberries and cream. Opposite: In 1946, Bobby is at right on the lower step along with fellow Harvard gridders (clockwise from there) John Fiorentino, Jim Noonan and Frank Miklos. He was probably the most accomplished of the Kennedy boys at football; Jack's best sport was golf, though as a politician he kept that fact hidden beneath a bushel since strategists said it was a Republican game.

ROBERT FRANCIS KENNEDY, born November 20, 1925, always wanted to be bigger and older than he was—always wanted the chance to do what Joe Sr. demanded of Joe Jr. and then Jack. In certain ways, he was the beneficiary of the rivalry between the two older brothers: Joe Jr. would lightly toss the football with Bobby for hours, and so would Jack, but between themselves a game like football would turn from touch to tackle, with no one announcing that it had. While Joe sensed a challenge from Jack (and the fun-loving Jack did nothing to dissuade him), Rose made sure her eldest sons treated the younger siblings with gentleness and compassion. Nevertheless, Bobby, smart and ambitious, applied himself with an intensity that was greater even than Joe Jr.'s and showed up at all the preordained stops: Harvard (where he lettered in varsity football, as neither of the older boys had); the military service (he entered the Navy's V-12 officer training program at Harvard in the spring of 1944, when he was 19, and later served on a ship named for his oldest brother); and finally politics. At one thing, he was first among the boys by a mile: On June 17, 1950, he married Ethel Skakel, and they built a family reminiscent in size of the turn-of-the-century Irish Catholic households we met earlier. Bobby and Ethel would have 11 children in all. Bobby was assassinated in 1968—and more on him, too, in a moment.

That's how the youngest child was always known in the family—certainly not Edward, and not even Ted, though the latter appellation is the one usually used when referencing the senator (now the late senator). "Teddy" it was, until the day he died. Those who became his inherited children—Caroline, John Jr. and all of Bobby's kids—called him Teddy more readily than Uncle Teddy. After he had walked Caroline down the aisle at her 1986 wedding, Caroline's mother, Jacqueline Kennedy Onassis, wrote him a letter that he treasured the rest of his life: "Dearest Teddy, Because of you, we're all going to make it." An interesting sentiment to express and not off the mark. The gregarious, fun-loving boy—the comic relief—who could be called nothing but "Teddy" grew into the paterfamilias, the dock to which all Kennedys anchored. At right, he is seen in the late 1930s with his oldest brother, Joe Jr., whom he saw as a hero and who, he later said, influenced him greatly. Opposite: A portrait with his father taken at about the same time. Just by the way: Another frame from the same portrait session is on the side table in the photograph on the last page of our book.

JEAN ANN KENNEDY, born on February 20, 1928, the little sister. She followed behind Eunice and Pat wherever they went. In London, when Joe was ambassador, the girls would trot off to convent school at Roehampton every Monday—Rosemary attended a special school in the English countryside at this time—and return to the official residence every weekend, happy with themselves and all the attention their comings and goings generated (the Kennedy kids were treated as celebrities during Joe's ambassadorship). In 1956, Jean married Stephen Smith, an executive with his family's New York transportation firm. As would the Shrivers, the Lawfords and, of course, the various Kennedys, the Smiths pitched in energetically during JFK's presidential campaign. In fact, Steve Smith became something of a rock for the Kennedy family, handling problems as they arose in any of the households and being a stable, trusted uncle to all the many nephews and nieces. Jean and Steve had raised four children together (two of them adopted) before Steve's death in August 1990. Jean Smith became the U.S. ambassador to Ireland in 1993, using her influence to forward the cause of peace.

EDWARD MOORE KENNEDY, born February 22, 1932, the little brother. To look at Ted Kennedy as we all regarded him in late August of 2009—the quintessential elder statesman, the old lion who focused attention once more on this remarkable family as he passed away—is to view the far end of a most remarkable transformation. He was once the boy in short pants, the puppy dog, the chubby-cheeked one in the corner of all the photographs. Then he was the handsome young man. Then he was the one who had to shoulder the cross. Then he was the one who seemed not quite up to it, the one who had problems with liquor, whose wife had problems with liquor, who was cheating and carousing in ways unseemly even for a Kennedy. Then he was the patriarch by default. Then he was on the verge of a last hurrah—maybe the presidency at last?—and he thundered back. Then he was the country's "last liberal," and as a Kennedy he was the unquestioned head of the family, the now enormous family. He was a large, weathered man who looked to be in his eighties, but in fact was not. He was, at the end, barnacled like few others in the country. More on him in a moment.

THOSE WERE THE MEMBERS OF THE Kennedys' famous generation. And how did they come to conquer the country?

That was father Joe's doing. Many, many books have been written about it, and it is our job here to briefly synopsize.

Joe Jr. was gone, the senior Joe was himself un-electable and so he would steer Jack's machine. He got support, of course, from John Fitzgerald—Honey Fitz was still going strong, and he certainly knew a thing or two about politics. But Joe was the boss.

In 1945, JFK and his father were eyeing the Massachusetts lieutenant governorship when, all of a sudden, Honey Fitz's old congressional seat came available. In the streets of Boston, Somerville and Cambridge, John F. Kennedy's remarkable charm and charisma were put on display. Young men signed up to support him; young women swooned. In 1946, Jack beat many comers and ascended to the same congressional seat his grandfather had held half a century earlier.

Years later, JFK as President would visit Ireland and be received as some triumphal general. Less well remembered, except by the family, was a trip he made there in 1947 to visit his sister Kathleen, who was staying at Lismore Castle in County Waterford. The estate belonged to the family of Kick's husband, Billy, who had died three years earlier. Lismore was a place the young widow considered "the most perfect" in the world. Goodwin quotes from Rose's diary and paints an image of the setting: "'A picture book castle' with its gray walls covered on one side with soft green moss and on the other with reddish ivy." Then "'the steep straight down drop to the quickly running stream . . . the artistic bridge over the stream with a few figures fishing and the winding road beyond where the children walk along from school in their bare legs and shabby shoes and torn coats but shining rosy faces.'"

We quote at a little length to make a point here: Almost precisely a century after Patrick Kennedy trudged the roads of Wexford, leaving an island of despair and death, Patrick's descendants, now of the ruling class in the world's suddenly ascendant nation, were able to revisit the homeland and see it as a pastoral idyll. Things had changed quickly for the Kennedys and the Fitzgeralds.

Jack thoroughly enjoyed his stay at Lismore and one morning enlisted Pamela Churchill, Winston's daughter-in-law, to accompany him on a pilgrimage in search of ancestors in the village of New Ross, 50 miles east. His Aunt Loretta had given him directions to the old family home. Here's Goodwin again: "They motored through the soft green countryside along the southeastern coast of Ireland and across the bottom of Kilkenny County, past wooded valleys and ruined castles, along roads so bumpy that it took more than five hours to reach the little market town of New Ross, settled on the banks of the Barrow River. At the outskirts of the town Jack stopped the car and asked a man where the Kennedys lived. 'Oh, now, and which Kennedys will it be that you'll be wanting? David Kennedys? Jim Kennedys?' a very Irish voice replied. Jack explained about being from America and looking for his relatives, and the man told him to drive to a little white house on the edge of the village."

They found the thatch-roofed domain and, Churchill reported later, "a tough-looking woman came out surrounded by a mass of kids, looking just like all the Kennedys." The woman finally softened, and the afternoon was spent in reminiscence and trying to figure out how they were related. (Third cousins was the upshot.) The family graciously offered butter and eggs, which no doubt would have been dear to them. Jack, on leaving, asked if he could do anything for them in turn. The woman asked if the children could have a ride around the village in the splendid station wagon. He gladly obliged, and it may have been one of the happiest, most moving times of his life.

During this visit to Ireland, while they walked by the banks of the Blackwater River, Kick confided to Jack that she had fallen in love with a married man, Lord Peter Fitzwilliam. The fact that she carried on an affair with him, that Peter was with her in the plane when she died, in no way lessened her brother's grief for his sister when she was gone less than a year later. Friends of the family were always pleased for both Kick and Jack that they had had that special time together at Lismore in 1947.

JFK dutifully served a couple of terms in Congress—he didn't seem engaged by the job, particularly, and spent more time socializing than legislating in Washington—and then, in 1952, he ran for the Senate. His father had been building a formidable statewide political operation in Massachusetts, and

INTO THE FRAY

Jack is only 29 in September of 1946, but he is a war veteran—a war hero—*whose older brother was killed in action, and he appears to the voters of Massachusetts like the future, hence the slogan at the top of this campaign poster. In his room at the Bellevue Hotel on Boston's Beacon Street, a hostelry steeped in tradition, where Louisa May Alcott lived when completing* Little Women, *Jack has made himself comfortable by placing pictures of his parents, representing his own heritage, on the mantel. It was not so very long before that the only Irish Catholics on Beacon Hill were working as maids in private mansions or as hired help in places such as the Bellevue. That one of them might now be seeking Honey Fitz's old seat in Congress was perhaps unsurprising, but that this young man might one day audaciously quest after the presidency was yet unthinkable. But that's what Jack's father, Joe, has squarely in mind, as was certainly clear to the rookie candidate, who once said about being asked—told—to take the absent Joe. Jr.'s place in public life: "It was like being drafted. My father wanted his eldest son in politics. 'Wanted' isn't the right word. He demanded it. You know my father."*

Jack knew the Senate was a place where he could better exercise his interests in foreign affairs. His opponent for the seat, the incumbent, stands as symbolic in much the same way that the visit to Ireland does: as an indicator of how things had changed so quickly. When the Kennedys were struggling in the North End of Boston along with all the other Irish, the Lodge family was already ensconced atop Beacon Hill. The isolationist Henry Lodge had defeated John Fitzgerald for the U.S. Senate 36 years earlier. Now it was grandson against grandson—John Fitzgerald Kennedy versus Henry Cabot Lodge II—and things were different.

Still, JFK entered the contest a heavy underdog. Joe Kennedy poured great amounts of his own money into the campaign and took over much of the decision making, sometimes to the consternation of his son. Suddenly arriving in Massachusetts was Bobby, who gave up his job at the Justice Department to join the campaign. Bobby worked both as a mediator between Joe and Jack and as a spark plug. He demonstrated previously unseen political instincts and energies. Kenny O'Donnell, a member of JFK's inner circle— his "Irish Mafia"—told Goodwin: "Those of us who worked with him over the next few months are convinced that if Bobby had not arrived on the scene and taken charge when he did, Jack Kennedy most certainly would have lost the election."

But he did not, and overnight this young prince was seen nationwide as a man who could, just possibly, be king.

Except . . . he was an Irish Catholic. The country would never elect a Catholic.

Times were good in America and John F. Kennedy looked the picture of good times. As a Most Eligible Bachelor—sort of the precursor title to *People* magazine's Sexiest Man Alive, a mantle that JFK's son would one day wear— Jack was right in tune with a Sinatra-sound-tracked *Mad Men* era. Ike was in the White House and that was okay—postwar stability, after all—but much of America found itself gently swinging. Jack Kennedy reflected what they wanted to see in the mirror, and when he married the beautiful Jacqueline Lee Bouvier on September 12, 1953, the country had to concede it had never set eyes upon a more attractive, more enviable couple. Image counts much in politics, and

no newlyweds have ever projected such an image as Mr. and Mrs. John Fitzgerald Kennedy. Drink them in for just a second as they sail off Cape Cod, and then think of Richard Nixon by contrast. That was the choice the country was faced with in 1960.

Again, of course, Kennedy was the underdog. The received wisdom was that Republicans would steer more cautiously through the nasty waters of the Cold War world. And, of course, JFK was Catholic.

Joe, who always played rough, played as rough as ever this time. One example shows how emphatically and desperately he wanted the White House, and this didn't involve any Irish Mafia of O'Donnell, Donahue and Powers; this involved the real deal. JFK was struggling in the Democratic primaries, and it looked like Texan Lyndon Johnson or some other candidate would be the nominee. The West Virginia primary would be crucial, and things didn't look good for Jack there—particularly because of the Catholic question in a non-Catholic state. It has been reported that Joe went to his son's friend Sinatra and asked if Sinatra could seek help from his friend, the mobster Sam Giancana. Sinatra said sure and intervened with Giancana. No quid pro quo, just a favor. Giancana got on the horn with the labor unions in West Virginia and, voilà, Kennedy won the primary. All such machinations were outshone, of course, by the high gloss of the campaign—Jack and Jackie smiling as the theme song "High Hopes" blared in the background, Frankie Boy singing a Kennedy-specific verse that he had asked his pal, the lyricist Sammy Cahn, to customize for the cause. Dirty business behind the scenes but in the spotlight razzmatazz.

It all worked, and history was made. In January of 1961, a son of a famine immigrant family was inaugurated as President of the United States of America. He became the de facto leader of the free world. "Ask not what your country can do for you," said John Fitzgerald Kennedy on that frigid day in Washington, "ask what you can do for your country."

Joe Kennedy, the father, was witness to the glory. Later that year, he suffered a stroke. Paralyzed, he would endure the murders of his second and third sons before dying on November 16, 1969, at age 81.

Well known are the salient details of JFK's presidency: his growing reliance on Bobby, Bobby's battles with labor and the Mafia (that certainly made

Giancana and Sinatra cheerful), the Bay of Pigs fiasco, the Cuban missile crisis triumph, the introduction of the Peace Corps, the escalation of military action in Vietnam, the early days of the civil rights movement and so much more that transpired during JFK's too-brief tenure in the White House. There's little point in recounting at any great length here the terrible events of November 22, 1963, and even less point in talking about conspiracy theories. The young President was killed, and his life passed into history and legend.

The main point, at this juncture, as we discuss dynasty: The Kennedys had climbed as far and high as one family can in this country, lifting its people's spirits as it went.

A second shining son of that family had been taken, and now the family marched on.

BOBBY PICKED UP THE MANTLE. OR, at least, he tried to—hesitantly at first. He challenged Republican Kenneth Keating for the New York Senate seat in 1964, suffering attacks from such as Gore Vidal and other liberals who labeled him a carpetbagger and formed Democrats for Keating. Bobby's heart wasn't in it at first, then Keating attacked him before an audience of Jews as linked with a "huge Nazi cartel," obviously trying to paint him as Joe's Jew-hating son. (The Justice Department under RFK had settled claims regarding the assets of General Aniline, a chemical company that was once tied to the Third Reich.) Keating's charge was a cheap shot, as was immediately evident to all, and Bobby shot back that one who had lost a brother and a brother-in-law in World War II could never be soft on Nazism. Outrageous, said Bobby of the charge. Now he was engaged, and he was on his way. That he won by 627,795 votes when presidential candidate Lyndon Baines Johnson defeated Barry Goldwater in New York State by more than two and a half million is more a comment on Goldwater than on Bobby Kennedy.

Still, after JFK's vivacity, made larger by memory, Bobby seemed serious, pointedly ambitious, hard. Fortunately for him, the times were about to get intense, even angry, and he would do more than tap into this, he would become a champion. Civil rights was already a significant issue for him, and after the Watts riots of 1966 in Los Angeles, he began a crusade for improvements in the inner city. As his Bedford-Stuyvesant Development and Services Corporation in New York City began to achieve tangible results, one black leader spoke for others: "Kennedy puts money where his mouth is." RFK's Migratory Labor Subcommittee looked into not only poverty in Appalachia but also the farm workers' exploitation in California. The committee became activist, and laws were changed. He became aware of the plight of New York's Native Americans and helped them. He became aware of the plight of laborers along the Mississippi delta and helped them. As Peter Collier and David Horowitz wrote in *The Kennedys: An American Drama,* "He went from one powerless group to another like a detective obsessively following clues to a mystery which he knew was inside himself. What was his responsibility to these people?"

He was becoming the left's shining star. Coming up on the outside as the liberal's principal cause—overtaking civil rights, overtaking the War on Poverty—was ending the conflict in Vietnam. Bobby took it up, and this put him in opposition to the Democratic President, his brother's former vice president, Johnson. When Democratic Senator Eugene McCarthy, riding the antiwar sentiment spreading throughout the land, made headway in early 1968 primaries by challenging LBJ, forces within the party started pressuring Kennedy to enter the race, saying that McCarthy was all well and good but unelectable, while Bobby looked very, very electable. Finally, RFK did throw his hat in the ring (those charges of opportunism were heard again), and his campaign was on the upswing when, after winning the crucial California primary on June 4, he confided to Kenny O'Donnell from his suite at the Ambassador Hotel in Los Angeles, "You know, Ken, finally I feel that I'm out from under the shadow of my brother. Now at least I feel that I've made it on my own. All these years I never really believed it was me that did it, but Jack."

After making his victory speech shortly after midnight at the Ambassador, he was ushered through the hotel kitchen, and for reasons still unfathomable, a man named Sirhan Sirhan gunned him down.

A third shining son of the family had been taken, and now the family marched on.

A TORCH TO BEAR
With Joe and Jack gone, there were two. In the photograph on the opposite page, the elder surviving brother, Bobby (right), is in McLean, Virginia, seeking the counsel of the younger, Ted, who in 1964 is a two-year veteran of the U.S. Senate, for which Bobby is making his maiden bid. Because Honey Fitz, Jack and Ted represented Massachusetts constituencies, and the family was linked inextricably to the Compound in Hyannis Port, charges of carpetbagging were leveled at Bobby when he determined to throw his hat into the ring for the seat from New York. But in fact, Joseph Kennedy had moved the family from Boston to the Gotham suburb of Bronxville many years before—even while maintaining the beloved retreat on Cape Cod—having chafed long enough under the imperious gaze of a Protestant aristocracy that still considered Irish Catholics an inferior class. Bobby won his election, of course, and within four years was tilting at the presidency. When he was taken from the stage, Ted tried to replace him. In some ways, he never could, and in others he surpassed both Jack and Bobby in accomplishments. When Ted died in 2009, he was celebrated as one of the best and most effective senators—and champions of the people—in the history of the country.

HAPPIER DAYS

Virginia Joan Bennett, who did some modeling as a teenager, was sought after by many men, among them Ted Kennedy. He had a reputation as a playboy, which was pretty much a de rigueur reputation for a male Kennedy, but she took her chances and married him in 1958. She was there with him for his earliest triumphs (as here when he ascends to the Senate) and stuck with him through the horrors of 1969. On July 18 of that year, at a cottage on Chappaquiddick Island off Martha's Vineyard in Massachusetts, Ted attended a reunion for six women who had worked for his late brother Bobby's presidential campaign. He left the party with a young woman that night and drove his Oldsmobile off the side of a bridge into Poucha Pond; he survived but she did not. It could not have been presaged with any certainty at the time, but Ted's presidential aspirations were finished. His marriage would not be for a while longer. Joan as well as Ted developed problems with alcohol, and their deteriorating union finally did end in 1982. Ted would marry again, in 1992, to Victoria Anne Reggie, who would help him back to health, stability and an energetic final chapter as the Senate's last liberal lion.

TED PICKED UP THE MANTLE. OR, AT least, he wanted to. He had been a senator from Massachusetts since 1962, even before Bobby had joined Congress. Now he was the surviving scion in a political dynasty and also, it could have been argued even back then, the paterfamilias. Joe Sr. had been taken off the field by his stroke (he would die a year and a half after Bobby), and the next generation, those who were now being called the "Young Kennedys," were not yet of age. (For politics, anyway. They were proving plenty old enough to start getting into trouble—of the misdemeanor kind, and of more serious consequence, too, as we will see). So there was Ted, and no one else.

The youngest brother said he was willing. At the tumultuous Chicago Democratic convention of 1968, Ted gave his first political speech since Bobby's death and offered candidly, "Like my brothers before me I pick up a fallen standard." There was talk of a draft at that convention, but Hubert Humphrey was the ultimate candidate (he would lose to Richard Nixon).

Things began to get strange: Jackie Kennedy, Jack's widow, married the Greek shipping magnate Aristotle Onassis, and the outcry in America was startling. Ted Kennedy returned to the Senate, but he was a troubled man—drinking too much, losing the focus that had made him a superb legislator. His wife, Joan, was also drinking. Still and all, Ted was regarded as a sure bet to be the 1972 Democratic presidential nominee.

TOOTHSOME
As the bad hair—the really bad hair—tells you, this photograph was taken in the 1970s, specifically 1972, during a family get-together in, yes, Hyannis Port. Rose, the grande dame, is in the center, and surrounding her are the grandchildren. This generation, too, would taste tragedy. One of Bobby's boys, David (fifth from right, back row), would die of a drug overdose in 1984, and David's brother Michael (top row, far right) would perish in a skiing accident in 1997. In 1999, John F. Kennedy Jr. (kneeling, far right), who was perhaps the young Kennedy most often pointed to as someone who was going to make his move, perished when the small plane he was piloting crashed into the Atlantic. His relations, including his sister, Caroline (top row, far left), did what Kennedys do: They mourned earnestly, and then they marched on.

Then, on July 18, 1969, after a party for a group of his brother Bobby's former campaign workers, the senator drove his 1967 Oldsmobile off Dike Bridge at Chappaquiddick on Martha's Vineyard. Though he escaped, his passenger, Mary Jo Kopechne, drowned in the bay. Kennedy was never found criminally responsible for the death, but Chappaquiddick would haunt him the rest of his life and would serve to derail his presidential aspirations.

It took a trial balloon or two for Kennedy to realize this truth, but truth it was. However, among the Massachusetts electorate, he was unbeatable, and so Ted Kennedy would evolve over the many years into a stalwart of the Senate and, also, the patriarch (now accepted by all) of the country's most famous family. Ted and Joan divorced in

1982 (and he later discreetly got an annulment). It took several more years, but Ted finally calmed down. In 1992, he married a smart lawyer named Victoria Reggie, and she helped him get in fighting trim for what promised to be a tough 1994 reelection campaign against the smooth, attractive Mitt Romney. It turned out to be another Kennedy landslide, not least because Ted's increasingly strong record as a legislator and public advocate was unassailable before the people of the Bay State.

Ted Kennedy's hair turned snow white, and he looked the part that had fallen to him but that he never would have chosen. He presided at the weddings and the wakes—most painfully, surely, at the memorial service of his cherished nephew John F. Kennedy Jr. in 1999.

TED JR. AND LEGACY

Right: On August 29, 2009, at his father's funeral, Ted Kennedy Jr. told a story about what informs the Kennedy ethos, and has for decades, and will tomorrow: "When I was 12 years old, I was diagnosed with bone cancer, and a few months after I lost my leg, there was a heavy snowfall over my childhood home outside of Washington, D.C. My father went to the garage to get the old Flexible Flyer and asked me if I wanted to go sledding down the steep driveway. And I was trying to get used to my new artificial leg, and the hill was covered with ice and snow and it wasn't easy for me to walk. And the hill was very slick, and as I struggled to walk, I slipped and I fell on the ice, and I started to cry, and I said, 'I can't do this.' I said, 'I'll never be able to climb that hill.' And he lifted me in his strong, gentle arms and said something I'll never forget. He said, 'I know you'll do it, there is nothing you can't do. We're going to climb that hill together, even if it takes us all day.' Sure enough, he held me around my waist, and we slowly made it to the top, and, you know, at age 12 losing a leg pretty much seems like the end of the world, but as I climbed onto his back and we flew down the hill that day, I knew he was right. I knew I was going to be okay. You see, my father taught me that even our most profound losses are survivable, and it is what we do with that loss, our ability to transform it into a positive event, that is one of my father's greatest lessons. He taught me that nothing is impossible."

He had seen it all, and toward the end the amazing thing seemed to be that all of it hadn't already been too much for him. And then he passed, after his battle with brain cancer, his other, last fight for universal health care yet to be won. He was mourned by everyone on both sides of the aisle.

THE KENNEDY POLITICAL DYNASTY, as considered by us and most Americans, has ended with Ted Kennedy's death. In 2008, Caroline Kennedy, Jack and Jackie's only surviving daughter (Arabella was stillborn in 1956), feinted at a U.S. Senate seat from New York but finally balked. Bobby Kennedy Jr. has oft been mentioned for higher office, but the activist lawyer has kept his focus on environmental matters and his college teaching position. Others of the next generation have, indeed, served in public office. Ted's son Patrick is a congressman from Rhode Island and Patrick's cousin Joe, another of Bobby's sons, once represented the 8th District in Massachusetts and is being mentioned as a possible candidate for his late uncle's Senate seat. Kathleen Townsend Kennedy, Joe's sister, was the lieutenant governor of Maryland, where her causes were education reform, community service and crime prevention, but she is now out of politics.

Politics is not the be-all and end-all, of course. The younger Kennedys—so many dozens of them now, and who knows which of them, or their own children, will choose what course— contribute to the fabric of the nation in many ways on a daily basis.

But politics was the route that Honey Fitz and then Joe Kennedy identified as the one to negotiate if the goal was achieving power and influence in America. Politics was the road Joe pointed his boys down. Politics led to John's ascension to the presidency and to Bobby's rise as a cultural hero. Politics was the path that Edward Moore Kennedy traveled for such a number of years toward his stature as one of the greatest legislators in the history of our republic.

And now he is gone.

And so we look at the Kennedys today and . . . Something is missing.

THEIR SAGA IN PICTURES

Now we have met the Kennedys. And next we revisit the extraordinary events that befell them as they reshaped American history.

THE GOLDEN ONES

These young men, the three who would make their family internationally famous, have the biggest smiles on Cape Cod as they pose at the Compound in Hyannis Port. There was nothing but optimism for Jack, Bobby and Ted as they looked to a limitless future, a future that had been opened for them by the achievements of their family's already remarkable past. Their family: Nothing meant more to them, or any Kennedy, than family. Said their father, Joe: "I tell them that when they end this life, if they can count their friends on one hand, they will be lucky. Stick

BOSS OF BEANTOWN

Above: A wood engraving that appeared in an English newspaper from 1850, right about the time the Fitzgeralds and the Kennedys were fleeing their homeland, depicts the chaos aboard an Irish immigrant ship. These vessels were overcrowded, unsafe and disease ridden; their reputation as "coffin ships" was notorious. But representatives of the two families made it across and would soon unite. Even before they did, the Fitzgeralds would conquer Boston. At the center of the photograph on the right, we see Mayor John Fitzgerald at a ceremony during Old Home Week in Beantown in July of 1908. Honey Fitz was the first person born to immigrants to be elected mayor of Boston. In the tight circles of the Hub's politics, he would become well acquainted with P.J. Kennedy, saloon owner and powerful East Boston ward boss, though he would have preferred distance between his daughter and P.J.'s son Joe. A footnote: The resplendently hirsute fellow at right in this photograph is the noted author and clergyman Edward Everett Hale.

HULTON/GETTY

ROSE IN CHARGE

John Fitzgerald finally did sanction the marriage of Joe Kennedy and his daughter Rose, which occurred in October of 1914 (above), and applauded more heartily when offspring began to issue. Just over nine months after their wedding, Joe and Rose welcomed Joe. Jr., and Honey Fitz, the ebullient new grandfather, crowed to the press that the parents had figured out their baby boy would, naturally, be a Harvard man, a business kingpin and a multiterm U.S. President. "Further than that," he said, "has not been decided." In the portrait at right, taken circa 1919, Joe Jr. is closest to his mother, Jack is next and Rosemary is the littlest one. Jack said much later that it was Rose who formed them in this period: "They talk a lot about Dad, but he was not around all that much. Mother deserves more credit than she gets. She is the one who was there. She is the one who read to us. She took us to Plymouth Rock and the other historic places. She gave me my interest in history." She could also be tough, as Ted later recalled: "Mother could have been a great featherweight. She had a mean right hand."

AP

THE KENNEDY INVASION

With all the antic merriment that the Beatles would display when storming New York a quarter century later, the young and even older Kennedys kicked up their heels in the highest style after Joe Sr. was posted to London by FDR in 1938. Opposite, top: Jack (left) and Bobby bid goodnight to their sister Eunice and their mother, Rose (below), on July 18, 1939, as the women depart the embassy for an important appointment at Buckingham Palace: Rose is to "present" her 18-year-old daughter to King George VI and Queen Elizabeth at the Court of St. James. The king himself is seen in the photograph at left along with Elizabeth, the future Queen Mum, flanked by their hosts, Rose and Joe Sr., at a party at the American embassy on May 11, 1939. Below: Teddy, being harassed by a pachyderm, and Bobby have functions and duties of their own to attend to in London: On June 9, 1938, they are part of the proceedings at the official opening of the Children's Zoo.

THE UNSINKABLE KENNEDYS

Whenever they gathered at the Cape, in that earlier era and subsequently, the energy level was off the charts, the action was fast, furious and often frivolous, and the rules were simple: fun in the sun. What became known as the Kennedy Compound was six acres of waterfront on Nantucket Sound and three houses belonging to Joe Sr., Jack and Bobby (other Kennedys owned property nearby). Joe had rented a cottage there in 1926 and bought the property three years later; it grew along with his family. LIFE's Alfred Eisenstaedt visited in the summer of 1940 and took pictures of roughhousing in the surf; Eunice winding up for a forehand as Jean, Bobby, Teddy, Joe Jr., Pat and Rose (seated in a chair) held their breath; and sailing (opposite, clockwise from left, Jean, Rose, Joe. Jr., Bobby, Pat and Eunice—and Teddy at the front). Left: Jack, upon returning from the war, unwound at the Compound in 1946. Although all the Kennedys loved the place, perhaps no one revered it as much as Ted, and he lived on the estate until his death. On August 27, 2009, in the wake of his passing, word floated that the Compound may be turned into a museum and education center.

WARTIME

Joe Jr., Kathleen and Jack seem earnest—and they are—as they walk, on September 3, 1939 (above), to Westminster to hear the British declaration of war against Germany. The lives of all three will be greatly changed. Joe, seen in pilot training at the Squantum Naval Air Station in Massachusetts on July 15, 1941 (top right), will be killed in action when his plane explodes over England in 1944. Jack, also a Navy man (far right, shirtless), will skipper the patrol boat PT-109 (opposite, top left), which will sink after a collision with a Japanese ship. He will save his crew when they are rescued in the Solomon Islands after he carves an SOS message into a coconut. (Jack, who had experienced ill health in his youth, will undergo many surgeries for his considerable injuries but will nonetheless be plagued by pain the rest of his life.) Kathleen, meanwhile, will fall in love with the rakish William Cavendish (opposite, top right), who will marry her before himself being killed in the conflict. Kick would die young, too, on May 13, 1948, when the plane in which she is traveling crashes (opposite, bottom).

COPIED BY ELLIOTT ERWITT/MAGNUM

REX USA

BETTMANN/CORBIS (2)

BOBBY STARTS A FAMILY

And it would be a big one, a really big one. It began, of course, with the nuptials. Top: On June 17, 1950, Bobby weds Ethel Skakel (top, at right) at Saint Mary's Roman Catholic Church in Greenwich, Connecticut, then poses during their reception at the Skakels' lavish estate with Bobby's sister Eunice, who is a bridesmaid. The babies start coming the next year, and they keep on coming: Kathleen in '51, Joe in 1952, Bobby Jr. in 1954, David in 1955 . . . and the 11th, Rory, in 1968—born after her father had been assassinated. But well before that awful year, there were happy times, joyous times. In these two other photographs, taken in 1957, Bobby douses Kathleen in the backyard pool in Virginia while Joe shouts with glee; and Bobby hoists Joe over his shoulders while Ethel howls with laughter. Once the raucous merrymaking had run its course, the members of the Kennedy household would end each night in prayer, the parents and their children on their knees. Jack, Bobby and Ted all imported the traditions of their own upbringings in various degrees of intensity, and the new generations of Kennedys would be drilled in piety and politics. And they would be told to care for one another.

PAUL SCHUTZER

LISA LARSEN

REX USA

JACK TAKES A BRIDE

In London in 1947, Jack was diagnosed with Addison's disease, a life-threatening adrenal gland deficiency that causes fatigue and weight loss. On the ship home, he became so ill that a priest was summoned to prematurely—and not for the last time—give Jack Kennedy his last rites. By the early 1950s, he had mastered silently bearing his many maladies and showing the public strength and vitality. As noted earlier, Jack challenged Henry Cabot Lodge II for his Senate seat in 1952 and won. Then he won the heart of Jacqueline Bouvier (opposite), the 23-year-old elder daughter of an upper-crust Catholic family from New York. Jackie was every bit Jack's match in wit, charm and intellect. She was private and soft-spoken but self-assured. Kennedy aide and biographer Arthur Schlesinger Jr. wrote that "underneath a veil of lovely inconsequence, she developed a cool assessment of people and an ironical slant on life . . . an all-seeing eye and a ruthless judgment and a steely purpose." Jack and Jackie wed in September of 1953, and the bridegroom's younger brothers flank him in this photograph taken in Newport, Rhode Island (above).

SWEET CAROLINE

The early years of the Kennedys' marriage were difficult. Jackie's penchant for spending lavishly on clothes perturbed Jack, and she found herself forced to apply grace and fortitude to a relationship in which she was constantly competing for her husband's attention against the demands of political life and his appetite for other women. Jackie suffered a miscarriage, then a stillbirth. Jack's chronic back problems worsened; the mere act of putting on socks or walking to the Senate chamber was for him, at age 37, excruciating. In 1954, he underwent major surgery to shore up his spine, despite a very real risk of death due to possible complications from his Addison's disease. He narrowly survived and began a seven-month recovery. In 1957, however, wonderful news, the best news: Caroline is born. The following year, Dad plays peekaboo in the Kennedys' Georgetown home (above), and in 1959, he and Mom enjoy the company of their daughter in Hyannis Port. All is right with the world.

BETTMANN/CORBIS

TED WEDS

After the family's rise in America, the Kennedys had little difficulty getting elite Catholic clergy to preside when sacramental rites were required. Young Teddy, through the intervention of his father, had received his first communion from Pope Pius XII, who had patted him on the head afterward and pronounced him a smart young fellow. In 1958, Ted was ready to get married, and on November 29, Francis Cardinal Spellman, archbishop of New York, commuted to suburban Bronxville to officiate the Nuptial High Mass at Saint Joseph's Church.

Older brother Jack was Ted's best man that day. Joan and Ted would settle in Squaw Island, Massachusetts, until Ted's 1962 election to the U.S. Senate. Opposite: They welcomed before then their daughter, Kara (in Dad's arms), in 1960 and son Teddy Jr. (in Mom's) the following year. Meantime, Ted and Jack and Bobby's sisters Eunice and Pat and Jean had started families of their own, and there were already well over a dozen next-generation Kennedys. Where this all might end, no one knew—and no one knows today.

THE GREAT CAMPAIGN

In his run for President in 1960, Jack proved himself a tremendous candidate—intelligent, eloquent and on point in explaining why his religion would not affect his policy making, cool under pressure during debates with Richard Nixon, charming when meeting with garden clubs and junior leagues. The army of Kennedy men and women fanned out across the land to boost him. In the photographs on this page, the Democratic standard-bearer, rising in the polls, reviews his speech before an appearance in Baltimore, then notices he has kibitzers. Opposite, in a Los Angeles hotel suite, he confers with his closest confidant, Bobby, who is managing the campaign. On the pages immediately following is an intense photograph taken by LIFE's Paul Schutzer, who covered the entire campaign (he took these Baltimore pictures) and was allowed into the Kennedy Compound on the decisive night. He was, he reported, "headquartered in a servants' bungalow between father Joe's, brother Bobby's and Jack's homes. As we watched the returns on TV and waited for a call to the command post in Bobby's house, we munched dainty cream cheese sandwiches provided by our hosts." The wait for a result in one of the closest elections of the 20th century was so pronounced, Schutzer was eventually allowed in to capture the tension. From left, keeping vigil, are Rose, Jack's adviser Ted Sorensen, Sargent Shriver, Jack's prep school classmate Lem Billings, Jean Smith, Stephen Smith and Peter Lawford.

HISTORY MADE

In a phenomenally tight election—the candidates separated by fewer than 120,000 votes of some 70 million cast—John F. Kennedy, at 43, became the youngest person and the only Catholic elected to the White House, as well as the first President to have been born in the 20th century. To a nation anxious about strife over civil rights, the Cold War and other issues, Kennedy's lofty inauguration day oratory offered hope, inspiration and an appeal to every individual's greater good. "Let the word go forth from this time and place, to friend and foe alike, that the torch has been passed to a new generation of Americans— born in this century, tempered by war, disciplined by a hard and bitter peace, proud of our ancient heritage, and unwilling to witness or permit the slow undoing of those human rights to which this nation has always been committed, and to which we are committed today at home and around the world." He urged his fellow Americans to "ask not what your country can do for you, ask what you can do for your country." The dynamism of that memorable, frigid inauguration day was captured for LIFE by a team of photographers including Ed Clark, who found Jackie clearly happy in her new environs (left, top); Joe Scherschel, who focused on the moment of the swearing in, with Jackie smiling and Rose in the background, left; and Paul Schutzer, who caught former President Harry S Truman giving Jack his John Hancock during the inaugural luncheon (left) and also, at day's end, the First Couple radiant at an inaugural ball (opposite). On the following pages, the President has taken up residence, his second child has been born, and Caroline and John F. Kennedy Jr., who is known to the world at large as John-John, run the Oval Office.

TED POLUMBAUM

MEANWHILE, THE OTHER BROTHERS

They were hardly biding their time during this period, and father Joe was still doing the steering. Bobby had performed wonderfully while managing Jack's campaign, but it still took arm-twisting from Dad, who could arm-twist with the best of them, for Bobby to be appointed Attorney General. Which he was, though Bobby later recounted that just before Jack trotted him out to the press he "told me to go upstairs and comb my hair, to which I said it was the first time the President had ever told the Attorney General to comb his hair before they made an announcement." Of course there were howls of protest, the word *nepotism* made familiar to all Americans—but the

Kennedys (or at least Joe) hardly cared. Bobby (opposite, in March of 1961) was a dogged AG, flinging elbows, kicking shins, making enemies. Ted was also in Washington now, working in an office apartment that was once Jack's (above, in February '61) and wondering what was in store. Dad knew. Ted ran for a Senate seat from Massachusetts in 1962, and of course there were howls of protest, the words *entitlement* and *chutzpah* made familiar to all Bay Staters. The Kennedys (or at least Joe) hardly cared. Ted won, at the minimally required age of 30, and began what would become the third longest career in U.S. Senate history—and one of the very most distinguished.

JOSEPH SCHERSCHEL

ALL PART OF THE RECORD

The duties of a President are many, and the activities of a President are observed minutely in their time. They are parsed by historians and theorists even more minutely in the years that follow—a President leaves legacies, intentional and unintentional, of many kinds. John F. Kennedy committed the country to space exploration and set a goal—which would be met—of landing a man on the moon by decade's end. Every space launch in the early 1960s, when the Cold War was at a fever pitch, was monitored in classrooms from coast to coast, and astronauts, particularly the members of the original Mercury 7, were heroes. None more so than John Glenn, the first American to orbit Earth on February 20, 1962, who is seen with President Kennedy on the page opposite inspecting his capsule, *Friendship 7,* shortly after the safe touchdown. A true hero as well was Eunice Shriver, Jack's sister, who, profoundly moved by the difficulties faced by their sibling Rosemary, was compelled to work with the mentally handicapped (above, at a children's home for the handicapped in Germany, in June of 1963). Now that she had a brother who was President, she had someone who could help her formalize her efforts, and so the National Institute of Child Health and Human Development was established. Of course, as we have said, there are all kinds of legacies, and one that lingers from the Kennedy years involves serious improprieties. At right is Marilyn Monroe standing between Bobby and Jack at a party, after having sung a sexy rendition of "Happy Birthday" to JFK at a celebration at Madison Square Garden in New York City. Jack had an affair with the actress, as he had with other women, precisely as his father had had affairs with actress Gloria Swanson and other women. Bobby, too, is rumored to have had a relationship with Monroe, and the most rabid conspiracy hounds wonder if the brothers were complicit in her death by drug overdose. These are the Kennedys. This is, for better or worse, a part of the Kennedy story.

CECIL STOUGHTON

FALLEN IDOL

The Kennedy family could not escape the grips of tragedy. Joe, who had worked so vigorously and at times ruthlessly to see his sons triumph, had precious little time to savor Jack's ultimate success. In December of 1961, he suffered a massive, disabling stroke and would be partially paralyzed if mentally lucid for the rest of his days. In August of 1963, Jackie gave birth to a third child (in fact, by the family's reckoning, a fourth; the girl, named Arabella, stillborn in 1956, was considered by them to have been the first). But Patrick Bouvier Kennedy was born prematurely with a respiratory disease and lived less than two days. At the funeral, the presiding prelate had

to coax the heartbroken President away from the tiny casket. And then, on the afternoon of November 22, 1963, the sword of Damocles fell once more on the Kennedys. During a trip to Texas to help seal a rift among local Democrats, the President and First Lady were riding through Dallas in a motorcade when gunshots rang out. Jack was hit in the head and neck and slumped over, his head resting in the lap of his wife as the limousine sped to the hospital. "Jack, Jack, can you hear me?" Jackie repeated as she bent over him, trying to support him. "I love you, Jack." Roughly half an hour later, at one p.m. central time, the President was declared dead. Jackie, in the immediate aftermath, would not change her bloodstained clothes: "I want them to see what they have done." On these pages are dramatic scenes from the day of the shooting and the days following. Opposite, top: A frame from the film made by Dallas dressmaker Abraham Zapruder, which was first revealed to the American public in the pages of LIFE. Above: On November 22, Bobby, at home in Virginia, is comforted by his children after learning what has happened. Left, center: The President's widow accompanied in the funeral cortege by (left to right) Stephen Smith, Bobby, Sargent Shriver and Ted. Opposite, bottom: John Jr. salutes his father.

THE FAMILY SPORT

Bobby and Ted would become surrogate fathers to John and Caroline after Jack's death, just as Ted would become the father figure for all of the three families' children once Bobby was killed. In the mid-1960s, the usual meeting places for the collected Kennedys included Hyannis Port, of course, and, when in Washington, RFK's Virginia estate, Hickory Hill. The property had been bought by Jack and Jackie in the 1950s, and after living there briefly, they sold it to Bobby and Ethel, who moved in with their burgeoning brood. If the house and its environs had been humming before, now it truly buzzed dawn to dusk. The Kennedys were famous for their touch-football games, which pushed the definition of *touch* to the extreme. "It's 'touch,'" a family friend recalled, "but it's murder." The contest seen here, with Bobby quarterbacking, is being staged during a break from a strategy session at Hickory Hill called by Bobby. This is his last weekend with his family in 1968 before he hits the presidential campaign trail, as he had made his fateful decision: "I can't be sitting around here calculating whether something I do is going to hurt my political situation in 1972. Who knows whether I'm going to be alive in 1972?" It is obviously painful to note in hindsight that these photographs represent one of the last cherished times he would spend at Hickory Hill. On the following pages, the magnetism that he commanded in the spring of '68 is on full display in the streets of Philadelphia.

BILL EPPRIDGE (2)

BOBBY IS TAKEN

While his brother Ted was recovering from a broken back suffered in a plane crash that had killed two others in 1964, Bobby had said, "I guess the only reason we've survived is that there are too many of us. There are more of us than there is trouble." This dark humor seems, in retrospect, chilling. His presidential campaign caught fire in '68 with a string of big victories in Indiana, Nebraska and, finally, California. There, shortly after midnight on June 5, RFK gave a victory speech (above) at the Ambassador Hotel in Los Angeles. Moments later, exiting through the kitchen, he stopped to shake hands with a busboy, Juan Romero. And then it happened: The moment Bobby had been vaguely anticipating for years. A man lurking in the crowd, 24-year-old Sirhan Bishara Sirhan, fired several shots from a revolver, hitting Bobby and, in the ensuing struggle, wounding five others. LIFE photographer Bill Eppridge, who had covered Bobby's campaign throughout, was there, and while everyone's attention was on the assailant, "there in front of me was the senator on the floor being held by the busboy. There was nobody else around, and I made my first frame, and I forgot to focus the camera. The second frame was a little more in focus . . . Then, just for a second . . . the busboy looked up, and he had this look in his eye. I made that picture, and then suddenly the whole situation closed in again. And it became bedlam." With a bullet lodged in his neck and another in his brain, Bobby underwent hours of surgery but never regained consciousness. He died early the next morning.

The casket was flown to New York City for a funeral, where Ted told the crowd, "My brother need not be idealized, or enlarged in death beyond what he was in life; to be remembered simply as a good and decent man, who saw wrong and tried to right it, saw suffering and tried to heal it, saw war and tried to stop it." His voice occasionally quavering, Ted closed with a quote Bobby used during the campaign, an adaptation of a line by George Bernard Shaw: "Some men see things as they are and say, 'Why?' I dream things that never were and say, 'Why not?'" As Bobby's casket slowly wended its way by train from New York to Washington, where it would be interred not far from Jack's body at Arlington National Cemetery (opposite, bottom), thousands upon thousands in the cities, towns and rural precincts spontaneously appeared along the route to salute, to cry, to wave goodbye (opposite, top).

BOSTON GLOBE/LANDOV

TED POLUMBAUM

CHAPPAQUIDDICK

For 36-year-old Ted, the sole surviving son, the darkness ahead was deep and devouring. "On you the carefree youngest brother," Jackie wrote him years later, "fell a burden a hero would have begged to be spared." He sought solace out on the open water, sometimes sailing through the night. Atop his own grief, Ted was now heir to an immense familial and professional burden, with all these newly father-less children and with politicos clamoring for him to leap into the campaign void left by his brother—entreaties that, in 1968, he rebuffed. By autumn, he returned to work, but he did not yet seem to be on anything resembling an even keel; on the flight home from an official trip to Alaska in 1969, reporters were surprised and concerned to see him rowdy, apparently drunk. Then came a weekend in July of that year that would alter the path of Ted's career and, for many, cast an eternal pall on his character. As mentioned earlier in our book, he attended a reunion on Chappaquiddick Island in Massachusetts for several women who had worked on Bobby's presidential campaign. He offered Mary Jo Kopechne a ride back to her hotel and proceeded to drive his Oldsmobile off the narrow Dike Bridge (opposite and above, after the car had been pulled from Poucha Pond). He said later that he managed somehow to escape; Kopechne did not. He also said he dove repeatedly into the water, trying in vain to save her, but of course there is no corroboration of his account. It was after nine a.m. the following day when Ted arrived at the police station to

JOHN LANDERS/BOSTON HERALD/POLARIS

file a report. By then, the car had been spotted belly-up in the water, police had been notified and the body of Kopechne had been extri-cated. A week later, Ted (above, at Dukes County Courthouse on Martha's Vineyard) pleaded guilty to leaving the scene of an accident and was given a suspended two-month jail sentence. Although Massachusetts voters would continue to elect him to the Senate for the rest of his life, Chappaquiddick would haunt him forevermore.

THE GOOD FATHER

When Edward Moore Kennedy Jr. spoke at his dad's funeral in Boston on August 29, 2009, those in attendance at the Basilica of Our Lady of Perpetual Help were profoundly moved—and justly so—by the story he told of his father taking him sledding (above: at it again in 1973, the year Ted Jr. lost his leg to cancer), a story that we recounted earlier, on page 38 of our book. But Ted Jr. said other things that day that are worth revisiting, too, as they shed light on what made his father such a survivor and, indeed, such an effective legislator: "He was a devout Catholic whose faith helped him survive unbearable losses and whose teachings taught him that he had a moral obligation to help others in need. He was not perfect, far from it. But my father believed in redemption, and he never surrendered. Never stopped trying to right wrongs, be they the results of his own failings or of ours." He went on later: "During the summer months when I was growing up, my father would arrive late in the afternoon from Washington on Fridays and as soon as he got to Cape Cod, he would want to go straight out and practice sailing maneuvers . . . And we'd be out late, and the sun would be setting, and family dinner would be getting cold, and we'd still be out there practicing our jibes and our spinnaker sets long after everyone else had gone ashore. Well, one night, not another boat in sight on the summer sea, I asked him, 'Why are we always the last ones on the water?' 'Teddy,' he said, 'you see, most of the other sailors we race against are smarter and more talented than we are. But the reason why we're going to win is that we will work harder than them and we will be better prepared.' And he wasn't just talking about boating." That day Ted Jr. called his father "my best friend." Opposite: The two of them in Moscow in 1974.

A future President inspects his property —

John Kennedy

THE DIFFICULTY OF BEING A KENNEDY

The family held to the biblical teaching that those who have been given advantages are required to give back, and certainly all the Kennedy children knew that much was expected of them. But while many thrived in this atmosphere and were in fact able to use their positions of privilege to contribute to society, others struggled with the pressures and, indeed, the pain of being a member of this blessed but so often ill-starred family. Several among the next generation of Kennedys had trouble with drugs or alcohol. David Kennedy, the fourth of Bobby and Ethel's 11 children, was an intelligent young teenager when, in 1968, he watched live coverage of his father's assassination on TV. He was obviously greatly affected; and whether this started his downward spiral, he began his recreational drug use not long after. In 1973, he was riding in a Jeep driven by his brother Joe that crashed; David's girlfriend was left paralyzed, and he suffered fractured vertebrae. He began using painkillers, and while still in prep school, he began using heroin. He wanted to be a journalist but eventually dropped out of Harvard and struggled mightily and in vain against his drug habit: He was hospitalized with an infection in 1976, and he overdosed two years later. He went into rehab in 1983 and reentered Harvard but stayed only a semester. He tried rehab again in early 1984, but during a family gathering in Palm Beach that Easter, he was found dead in his hotel room from yet another overdose. He was the first of his generation of Kennedys to die in adulthood, but he has not been the last. Above: Joe is David's lead pallbearer at Hickory Hill. Opposite: A portrait of young David that was taken by First Lady Jackie Kennedy in 1962 and that, today, is exceedingly poignant because of the inscription on it by President Kennedy, which reads, "A future President inspects his property."

STEVE LISS/GETTY

WEDDINGS AS WELL AS WAKES

There has been much joy as well as sorrow for the younger Kennedys. They grew, they married, they had children of their own. At left, we have the wedding of Caroline Kennedy to Edwin Schlossberg on July 19, 1986, at Our Lady of Victory in Centerville, Massachusetts, her cousin Maria Shriver serving as matron of honor this day and her uncle Ted walking her down the aisle. On the opposite page, we have the nuptials of John F. Kennedy Jr. and Carolyn Bessette on September 21, 1996, on Cumberland Island, Georgia, his older sister, Caroline, the matron of honor this time and his cousin Anthony Stanislas Radziwill serving as best man. After the death of their father when they were little, both Caroline and John grew to be sterling young adults under the loving guidance of their mother, Jackie. Both became lawyers; Caroline has written and edited books, including two she co-wrote on the subject of civil liberties, while John was the founding editor of the now-defunct political magazine *George*. Caroline has two daughters and a son of her own and, like her mother before her, has been involved in a number of civic causes in New York City. Throughout the 1990s, there was near constant speculation, of course, that one or both of these bright, energetic, attractive Kennedys might enter politics, and there was nothing invalid in the speculation; each of them certainly looked electable. But neither made a move. We will never know what achievements might have awaited John, for on July 16, 1999, he was at the controls of a small plane headed for Martha's Vineyard when it crashed off the Massachusetts coast. John's wife and his sister-in-law, Lauren Bessette, died with him. Caroline was bereft; she and her brother had always been close. It fell to Ted to deliver the eulogy for his departed nephew, and he did so with eloquence, grace and wit. He rightly credited Jackie for the job she had done with her son: "When they left the White House, Jackie's soft and gentle voice and unbreakable spirit guided him surely and securely to the future. He had a legacy, and he learned to treasure it. He was part of a legend, and he learned to live with it." Ted also told a truly funny story: "Once, when they asked John what he would do if he went into politics and was elected President, he said, 'I guess the first thing is call up Uncle Teddy and gloat.' I loved that. It was so like his father."

DENIS REGGIE

SURVIVORS

On July 23, 1982, the Kennedys and friends gather in Hyannis Port to celebrate Rose's 92nd birthday, and Ted is again—of course—called upon to speak. The remarkable Rose will live yet another dozen years before dying at the age of 104, and Ted still has another good quarter century ahead of him—the only Kennedy brother of his generation to be allowed his fair share of years. It can be said that, with the exception of occurrences like John Jr.'s premature death, this last period of Ted's life proved to be one of the best. Certainly in terms of political accomplishment, it was tremendous; both sides of the aisle acknowledge that Kennedy's work ethic and stoic faith in his principles and philosophies bolstered one of the most successful legislative careers ever. With his death, the opinion was voiced by many, if not all, that Ted, as a public servant, had outshone his brothers. And personally, too, Ted enjoyed great good fortune in his senior years. The Reggie family of Louisiana was involved for many a year in Democratic politics, and the Reggie and Kennedy families were friends. In June of 1991, Ted was at the 40th wedding anniversary celebration for Edmund and Doris Ann Reggie, when he started talking to their daughter, Victoria Anne, herself a smart, politically engaged lawyer. Ted later recalled, "I had known Vicki before, but this was the first time I think I really saw her." They wed the following year, and Vicki is widely credited with helping Ted find his better self, avoiding the vices and concentrating on work, family and the good things in life. On the pages that follow are scenes from Ted's final chapters: First, sailing off the Cape, which always gave him the greatest pleasure. Then, the most senior of statesmen, walking on the White House grounds with President Barack Obama, whom Kennedy had enthusiastically supported during the 2008 election. And finally, Hyannis Port yet once more, as the late senator's casket is borne by an honor guard.

FAREWELL

"For all those whose cares have been our concern,
the work goes on, the cause endures, the hope still lives,
and the dream shall never die."

—EDWARD M. KENNEDY, AUGUST 12, 1980

VICKI, TED AND THEIR DOG SPLASH IN WASHINGTON, D.C., IN FRONT OF A PORTRAIT OF JOSEPH P. KENNEDY, MAY 2009